Phonics Plus, Ki

Content

Contents Continued

Introduction

Learning to read can be a difficult task. Recent research indicates that many children are struggling as they try to grasp the rudiments of a confusing system of letters, sounds, and words. The United States government grew concerned by the number of children emerging from school who lacked a reading foundation and comprehension skills. In response, Congress issued a mandate that no child should be left behind in the classroom. As a result, teachers, children, parents, and government are working together to make sure that every child becomes a successful reader.

The National Reading Panel (NRP), a group of educators selected to act on behalf of the government, reviewed numerous reports and studies to determine the important elements essential to reading success. In 2001, the panel published *Put Reading First: The Research Building Blocks for Teaching Children to Read.* The report identified five areas critical to reading development: phonemic awareness, phonics, vocabulary, fluency, and comprehension.

The Five Reading Essentials

 • **Phonemic Awareness** involves hearing and identifying the individual sounds, or phonemes, in words and understanding that sounds can be manipulated to create new words.

 • **Phonics** focuses on the letters of the alphabet and their relationship to spoken sounds.

 • **Vocabulary** refers to the words that we hear, speak, read, and write that help us communicate.

 • **Fluency** is the ability to read a text silently or orally with accuracy and speed.

 • **Comprehension** is being able to understand the words and the purpose of a selection.

While the NRP identified five separate areas of reading instruction, it also determined that all five skills need to be taught in conjunction with one another to further ensure reading success.

The Phonics Series

This reproducible phonics series supplements many recognized phonics programs, yet still implements the other four reading elements identified by the NRP. As a phonics series, the information is presented in a systematic order and provides explicit instruction. Each unit contains phonemic awareness activities for the key phonics skill. Moreover, each phonics skill is supported with a small booklet that children can make and read. Vocabulary, fluency, and comprehension development activities help to further reinforce the phonics skill.

Organization of *Phonics Plus*

This book is divided into four units. The first unit focuses on readiness skills. The second unit deals with alphabet recognition of partner letters. The third unit provides practice in the letter and sound relationships of the consonant letters. In unit four, children explore the short vowel sounds. The unit components are explained below.

• **Planner** A chart at the beginning of each unit outlines the phonics skills and activities that can be completed during the unit. The chart formatting is easy to read and can be reviewed quickly to note the activities accompanying the unit. It identifies phonemic awareness activities, a skill-specific phonics activity, the vocabulary words for the related story, and the name of the story. Moreover, the planner lists familiar stories, songs, and nursery rhymes that can be used to introduce or reinforce each letter and sound.

• **Teacher Information** A two-page spread following the planner provides explicit instructions for completing the activities listed in the planner. A section is devoted to phonemic awareness activities and phonics activities. The information also guides activities to be used prior to reading, during reading, and after reading the unit story. These ideas support the essential skills of fluency, vocabulary, and comprehension. The teacher information also provides writing ideas to support creative use of words. Finally, these pages suggest activities that will help children apply their knowledge of phonics as they share the unit story at home.

- **Phonics** Activity pages blend the familiar skill pages with fun activities consisting of mazes, crossword puzzles, and coloring. On many pages, children have the opportunity to write a sentence so they are applying phonics skills in a new format.

- **Vocabulary** Three of the units have a page that explores some of the words in the unit story. The words were chosen to support a specific vocabulary skill. You may also wish to review the story in advance to select other words children may find challenging.

- **Story** A story was selected to support the phonics skills in each unit. You can duplicate the eight-page story so that each child can have a personal copy. Each phonics skill is included in the story, and the skill words are noted on the teacher information component.

Other Components

- **Phonemic Awareness Interview** An oral assessment can be found on pages 5–10. The Phonemic Awareness Interview gauges children's ability in four tasks: the ability to tell whether the beginning sounds (phonemes) in words are the same or different, the ability to produce the initial sound in words, the ability to blend isolated sounds to form words, and the ability to segment individual sounds in words.

- **Blackline Masters** The planner suggests fun, hands-on activities that support each phonics skill, such as creating word slides or flip books. The patterns for these activities can be found on pages 153 through 157. The teacher information component details how to use the blackline masters.

- **Writer's Dictionary** A dictionary page can be found on page 157. Several activities suggest that children write words or draw pictures whose names contain a phonics sound in the Writer's Dictionary. It is suggested that you make a 26-page personal "dictionary" for each child using this page. Have children color the letter in the margin to show the alphabet page in their dictionary. Additional pages can be copied and inserted if children need more room to write and draw.

We hope you enjoy this new and exciting phonics product. It is sure to complement any phonics program you choose!

How to Assemble the Stories

1. Reproduce the story pages as they appear in this book. For each story: photocopy pages 2/7 on the back of pages 8/cover; photocopy pages 4/5 on the back of pages 6/3.

2. Place pages 4/5 on top of pages 2/7.

3. Fold the story in half so that pages 4/5 face each other and the cover is on the outside.

4. Staple the book together along the outer left edge.

Phonemic Awareness Interview

The Phonemic Awareness Interview is an oral test designed to provide informal assessment of a child's level of phonemic awareness to help you plan for the development of literacy activities.

General Directions for Administering

The Phonemic Awareness Interview should be conducted individually in a quiet and comfortable setting. By administering the Interview individually, the teacher can be sure the child is attending to the task and can gain insights into problems the child may be having.

You may use any one, or all, of the tasks. If you wish to obtain a comprehensive understanding of the child's phonemic awareness, administer all four tasks. If you are interested in evaluating a specific aspect of phonemic awareness, administer only those tasks that are relevant to your needs. Whether you administer all four tasks or just selected tasks, the tasks should be given in sequential order.

There is no time limit. However, a period of 15 to 20 minutes is suggested to administer all four tasks. If possible, the tasks should be administered in a single session.

You and the child should be seated at a flat table or desk. The best seating location for you is facing the child, to facilitate clear diction and immediate recording of responses.

Become familiar with the directions and items. Specific directions for administering each task can be found on each "Administering and Recording Form." The text in **bold** type is intended to be read aloud. The other information is for the teacher only and should not be read aloud. You should feel free to rephrase the directions, to repeat the samples, or to give additional examples to make sure the child understands what to do.

Before beginning the Interview, spend a few minutes in light, friendly conversation with the child. Don't refer to the Interview as a "test." Tell the child you would like to play some "word games."

Specific Directions for Administering

Follow these steps to administer the Phonemic Awareness Interview:

1. Duplicate a copy of the "Administering and Recording Form" on pages 7–10 for each task you will be administering and one "Summary of Performance Form" on page 6. You will record a child's responses on the "Administering and Recording Form" and summarize the totals on the "Summary of Performance Form." The child will not need any materials.

2. Explain that the words the child hears and says every day are made up of sounds and that you will be saying some words and sounds and asking questions about them. Be sure to speak clearly.

3. Administer the tasks in sequential order. If the child has difficulty with the first few items or cannot answer them, you may wish to discontinue conducting that particular task until a later time. If the child misses half of the items on any task, move on to the next task.

4. Follow the same basic procedures when administering each task. First, model the task so the child understands what to do. Second, administer the sample item and provide positive feedback to the child. Third, administer the items for that task. Fourth, record the child's responses for each item.

5. After the Interview, record the child's scores on the "Summary of Performance Form." Use the "Level of Performance" scale on the "Summary of Performance Form" to determine the level that best describes the child's understanding of phonemic awareness. Children whose scores reflect minimal or emerging understanding may need additional oral language experiences. You may also wish to record specific observations from the Interview, especially for those areas where the child had obvious difficulty with the task or required additional prompting.

Phonemic Awareness Interview

Name _____ Grade _____ Date _____

Summary of Performance Form

Task	Score	Comments
Task 1: Sound Matching	_____/8	_____
Task 2: Sound Isolation	_____/8	_____
Task 3: Sound Blending	_____/8	_____
Task 4: Sound Segmenting	_____/8	_____
Total Phonemic Awareness	_____/32	_____

Level of Performance (circle one):

Minimal	Emerging	Strong
0–12	13–25	26–32

Comments:

Phonemic Awareness Interview

Task 1: Sound Matching
Administering and Recording Form

Task: The child will listen to two words and will indicate if the two words do or do not begin with the same sound.

Model: I am going to say two words. Listen carefully so you can tell me if the two words begin with the same sound: *monkey, mother*. Listen again: *monkey, mother*. The words begin with the same sound. *Monkey* and *mother* begin with the same sound.

Sample: Listen to these two words: *rain, snow*. Listen again: *rain, snow*. Do the two words begin with the same sound? (no) You're correct. *Rain* and *snow* do not begin with the same sound.

Now listen to some more words. Tell me if the words begin with the same sound.

Name _____ Grade _____ Date _____

Items	Circle child's response. (Correct response is underlined.)	
1. leg, lunch	<u>Same</u>	Different
2. duck, pan	Same	<u>Different</u>
3. sun, moon	Same	<u>Different</u>
4. fork, fish	<u>Same</u>	Different
5. chocolate, checkers	<u>Same</u>	Different
6. phone, poem	Same	<u>Different</u>
7. ball, banana	<u>Same</u>	Different
8. red, net	Same	<u>Different</u>

Total Score: _____/8

Comments:

Phonemic Awareness Interview

Task 2: Sound Isolation
Administering and Recording Form

Task: The child will listen to a word and then will produce the initial phoneme in the word.

Model: **I am going to say a word. Then I am going to say just the beginning sound. Listen carefully for the beginning sound:** *pig*. **The beginning sound is /p/.**

Sample: **Listen to another word. This time, you tell me the beginning sound. Listen carefully:** *goat*. **What is the beginning sound in** *goat*? (/g/) **You're correct. /g/ is the beginning sound in** *goat*.

If the child tells you a letter name, remind the child to tell you the *sound*, not the letter.

Now listen to some more words. Tell me the beginning sound you hear in each word.

Name _____ Grade _____ Date _____

Items	Correct Response	Child's Response
1. dot	/d/	_____
2. map	/m/	_____
3. sad	/s/	_____
4. talk	/t/	_____
5. cow	/k/	_____
6. bird	/b/	_____
7. farm	/f/	_____
8. yellow	/y/	_____
Total Score: _____/8		

Comments:

Phonemic Awareness Interview

Task 3: Sound Blending
Administering and Recording Form

Task: The child will listen to individual sounds and will blend the sounds together to say the word.

Model: I am going to say some words. Then I want you to put the sounds together to make a word. I will do the first one. Listen to the sounds: /r/-/u/-/n/. When I put the sounds /r/-/u/-/n/ together, they make the word *run*.

Sample: Listen to these sounds: /k/-/a/-/t/. What word do you make when you put /k/-/a/-/t/ together? (cat) You're correct. The sounds /k/-/a/-/t/ make the word *cat*.

Now listen again. I will say some sounds. You put the sounds together to make a word and tell me the word.

Name _____ Grade _____ Date _____

Items	Correct Response	Child's Response
1. /g/-/ō/	go	_____
2. /sh/-/ē/-/p/	sheep	_____
3. /j/-/u/-/m/-/p/	jump	_____
4. /a/-/n/-/t/	ant	_____
5. /h/-/o/-/t/	hot	_____
6. /l/-/i/-/p/	lip	_____
7. /d/-/e/-/s/-/k/	desk	_____
8. /b/-/ī/	by	_____
Total Score: _____/8		

Comments:

Phonemic Awareness Interview

Task 4: Sound Segmenting
Administering and Recording Form

Task: The child will listen to a word and then will produce each phoneme in the word separately.

Model: **I am going to say a word. Then I am going to say each sound in the word. Listen carefully for each sound. The word is *go*. The sounds in *go* are /g/-/ō/.**

Be sure to articulate each sound separately. Do not simply stretch out the word.

Sample: **Listen to this word. This time, you tell me the sounds in the word. Listen carefully: *man*. What sounds do you hear in *man* ?** (/m/-/a/-/n/) **You're correct. The sounds in the word *man* are /m/-/a/-/n/.**

Now listen to some more words. Tell me the sounds you hear in these words.

Name _____ Grade _____ Date _____

Items	Correct Response	Child's Response
1. dog	/d/-/ô/-/g/	_____
2. keep	/k/-/ē/-/p/	_____
3. no	/n/-/ō/	_____
4. that	/th/-/a/-/t/	_____
5. me	/m/-/ē/	_____
6. do	/d/-/oo/	_____
7. race	/r/-/ā/-/s/	_____
8. in	/i/-/n/	_____
Total Score: _____/8		

Comments:

Unit I Planner
Readiness

Lesson	Phonemic Awareness	Phonics A B C	Vocabulary	Comprehension and Fluency	Stories, Songs, and Rhymes
Lesson 1 Listening for Details	**Phoneme Isolation:** Isolate beginning sounds of target words from oral directions.	Listen to a Story Activity Page 14			**Story:** "Goldilocks and the Three Bears"
Lesson 2 Visual Discrimination	**Phoneme Categorization:** Recognize the target words that have the "odd" sound. *bus, bun, rug* *lit, zig, lick* *fat, flag, gas*	Finger Puppets Activity Pages 15–21			**Song:** "Hokey Pokey"
Lesson 3 Motor Skills	**Phoneme Segmentation:** Break target words into separate sounds, clapping each sound. *flag, dad, mop, pig*	Step-Page Book Activity Pages 22–26			**Song:** "If You're Happy and You Know It"
Lesson 4 Auditory Discrimination	**Phoneme Manipulation:** Substitute beginning sounds for target words. *bat, dog, tan*	Word Ladders Activity Page 27			**Nursery Rhyme:** "Little Boy Blue"
Lesson 5 Story: "The Cat"			*cat, box, gate, slide* Activity Page 28	Story Pages 29–32	

Phonics, Kindergarten SV 8860-9

Unit 1: Readiness

🐦 Develop Phonemic Awareness

The focus of this unit is to review readiness skills in connection with introducing letter shapes. However, it is recommended that teachers play daily sound games with children to develop attentiveness, listening skills, and initial recognition of the letter sounds.

• **Phoneme Isolation** As you read oral directions, have children listen for details. Then select a word from the directions and have them isolate the beginning sound of that word.

• **Phoneme Categorization** Have children practice identifying which objects and/or letters are the same and different. Then use the target words in the planner on page 11 and challenge them to recognize the "odd" sound.

• **Phoneme Segmentation** Have children break target words from the planner into separate sounds, clapping for each individual sound. Then encourage them to write down the letter for each sound they heard. Emphasize that words are written from left to right.

• **Phoneme Manipulation** Review rhyming words by having children substitute beginning sounds for the target words in the planner. Make a list on the chalkboard or a chart as each child names a different sound to be substituted for the target word. Have children help you read all the rhyming words on the list.

🔤 Explore Phonics

Use these group activities to help children use readiness skills to practice identifying letter shapes and their sounds.

• **Listen to a Story** Encourage children to listen for details as you read a brief story. Select a target word from the story. Challenge children to identify the beginning sound in the target word. Example: Select the word *sun* from the directions on page 14. Ask: *What is the beginning sound of* sun? You may wish to have children write the letter that makes the beginning sound and draw a picture of the target word.

• **Finger Puppets** Provide copies of Master 1 on page 155. Have each child make two finger puppets. Have children draw a happy face on one puppet and a sad face on the other. Make a set of cards that have two letters on each card. Write the same two letters on some cards and two different letters on others. Display one card at a time. Have children wiggle the happy face puppet if the letters are the same and the sad face if they are different. Encourage children to name an object that begins with the sound of the letter or letters shown.

• **Step-Page Book** Provide each child with a copy of Master 4 on page 156. Once the books are assembled, say each of the target words from the teacher planner. Repeat the first word. Then have children break the word into separate sounds. Challenge them to write each sound they hear on the first page of their book. Repeat the process with each target word using the remaining pages. Have them draw pictures or cut pictures from magazines that illustrate each of the target words.

• **Word Ladders** Write one of the target words from the teacher planner on a card. Place the word card on the base of a wall. Make a set of letter cards using various consonants. Choose one child at a time to select a card. Have the child identify the letter, substitute the letter sound with the beginning sound of the target word, and say the new word. Challenge children to write the new word on a card and tape it on the word ladder. Repeat the process with the remaining target words.

📖 Develop Vocabulary and Meaning

Position Words
down, in, out, over, under, up

High-Frequency Words
can, did, go, he, in, is, of, the, where

Story Words
cat, box, slide, gate

The following activities will help prepare children for reading the unit story independently. Afterwards, children can complete the vocabulary exercise on page 28.

- **Match the Words** Write one of the story words on the chalkboard and read it aloud. Circle the initial consonant, name the letter, and repeat the word, stressing the beginning sound. Repeat the process and have children echo. Then challenge children to find the word and circle it in their book. Repeat the process for each story word.

- **Find It** Write the vocabulary words on sentence strips. Introduce each word by reading and spelling it. Have children echo read and spell each word. Then invite volunteers to tape each sentence strip to an object in the room that has the same beginning sound as the vocabulary word.

Read the Story: "The Cat"

Before Reading

Invite children to look at the cover of the book. Encourage children to comment on whom the story is going to be about. Tell them that the cat likes to go to many different places. Read the story aloud. Invite children to follow along in their books and listen for the places that the cat goes.

During Reading

- **Model Fluency** As you read the story aloud, model the fluency skill of observing pauses indicated by periods.

- **Model Decoding** You may wish to model how to decode words using phonics sounds.

- **Model Comprehension** You may wish to model how to understand the story by pausing before reading a sentence and asking how the illustration helps the reader understand a story word.

After Reading

Have children find and read the words or phrases in the story that answer the following questions.

Whom was the story about? (a cat)

What did the cat get in? (a box)

What did the cat climb up? (a slide)

What did the cat go under? (a gate)

Why is the cat hiding behind the bush? (Answers will vary. Accept all reasonable answers.)

Reread the Story

- **Oral Reading** Invite children to take turns reading aloud lines from the story. Encourage them to read from left to right using a finger to point to each word as it is read.

- **Fluent Reading** Have partners turn to page 2. Point out that the sentence ends in a period. Explain that this ending mark tells the reader when to stop reading. Model how to read the sentence. Invite partners to take turns reading sentences and stopping at the periods.

- **Retell the Story** Ask children to tell what happens in the story in their own words. Encourage them to tell the story as a narrative, using picture details to help them recognize the sequence of events.

Connect the Story to Writing

- **Illustrate a Sentence** Invite children to choose a sentence from the story, write it on a piece of paper, and then draw their own picture to illustrate it. Reread the story, and as you read each sentence, have the children who illustrated that sentence share their work.

- **Innovate on the Story** Invite children to use their imagination and think of other places where the cat might go. Have them write and illustrate a sentence about a place the cat goes. You may wish to have children dictate their sentence to you, depending on ability level.

 Support ESOL Learners

Children who are learning English may have difficulty with the meanings of some of the story words. Teachers should provide daily practice with letter recognition and letter sounds with activities such as songs or finger plays.

At Home

Encourage children to read "The Cat" with someone at home. Suggest that after reading the story they name places that they have seen their cat or some other cat go.

Name _____

Outdoor Fun

■ Have children listen as you tell them what to do: Color the sun yellow. Color the rabbit brown.
Color the fish orange. Draw a bird in the nest. Draw a fishing pole in the boy's hands.

Phonics, Kindergarten SV 8860-9

Name _____

Toy Store

■ Have children color the two toys on each shelf that are the **same**.

Name _____

Dinner Time

■ Have children color the bowl in each set that looks **different**.

Phonics, Kindergarten SV 8860-9

Name _____

Home in a Shoe

■ Have children circle the children who are playing **outside** the shoe. Then have them color the picture.

Soapbox Derby

■ Have children color each child who is **inside** a car.

Name _____

What's Missing?

■ Have children draw the missing parts to make each picture pair the same.

Name _____

Signs of Spring

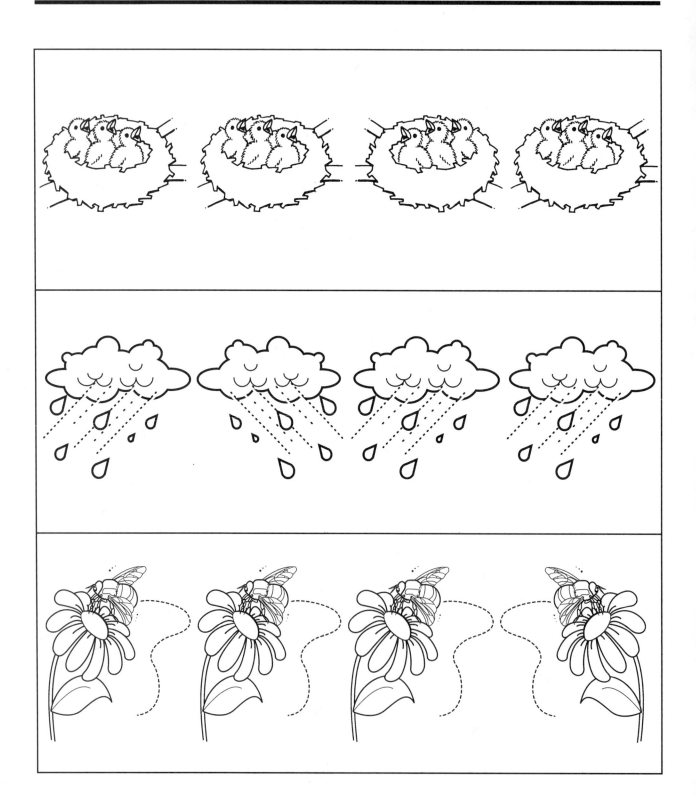

■ Have children circle the picture that is **different** from the others.

Phonics, Kindergarten SV 8860-9

Fun and Games

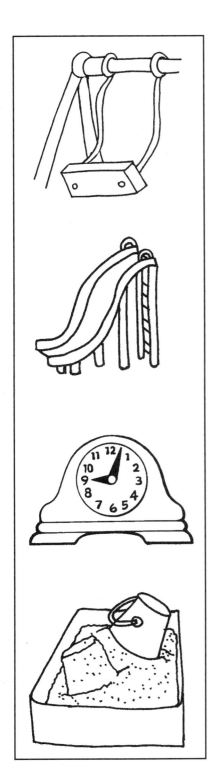
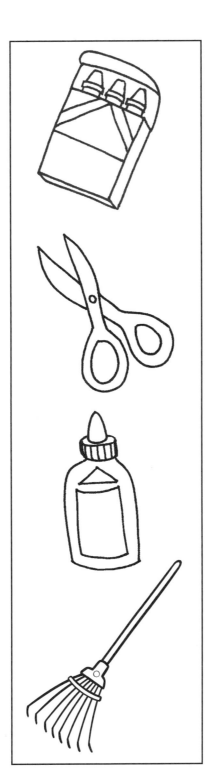
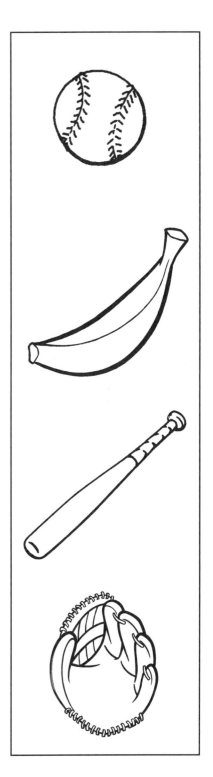

■ Have children color the pictures in each box that belong together.

Name _____

Home Sweet Home

■ Have children put their pencil on the dot beside the animal. Then have them lead the animal home by tracing the dotted line.

Unit 1: Left to Right

Phonics, Kindergarten SV 8860-9

Name

Hang on Tight

■ Have children put their pencil on the dot below each balloon. Then have them trace the line down to the one who is holding the balloon. Invite children to color the balloon and T-shirt the same color.

Unit 1: Top to Bottom

Phonics, Kindergarten SV 8860-9

Name

Shoots and Roots

■ Have children color the parts of the plants that are growing **above** the ground.

Unit 1: Above
Phonics, Kindergarten SV 8860-9

Name _____

Below the Sea

■ Have children color the pictures and cut them out. Then have them glue the animals that live **below** the ship in the empty boxes.

Name _____

Carefree Cubs

■ Have children put their pencil on each dot and trace the dotted lines to complete each picture. Have them follow the arrows. Invite children to color the picture.

Name

Rhyme Time

■ Have children color the pictures that rhyme with the picture on the left.

Phonics, Kindergarten SV 8860-9

Name _____

Vocabulary

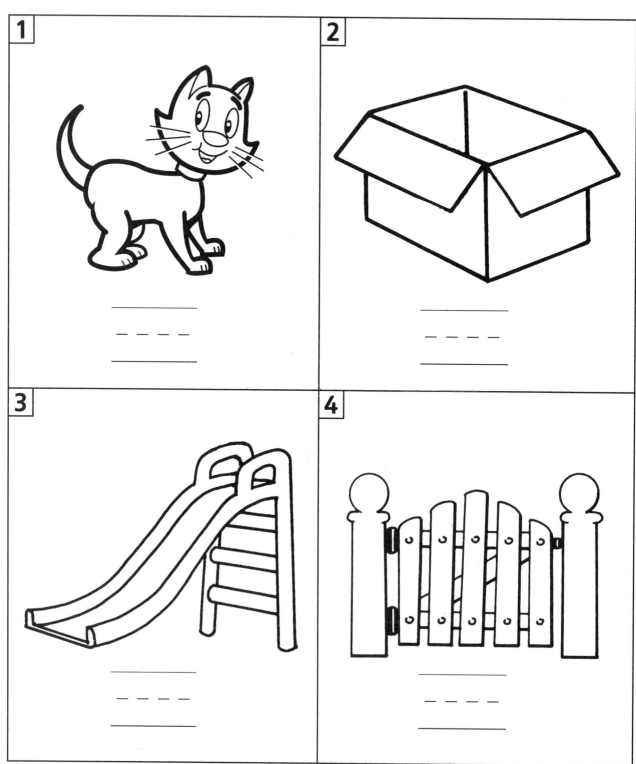

■ Have children name each picture. Then have them write the beginning sound of each picture name.

The Cat

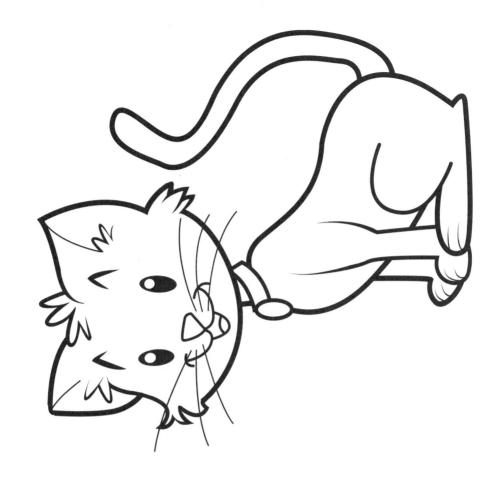

Where did the cat go?

He is in the box.

He is under the gate.

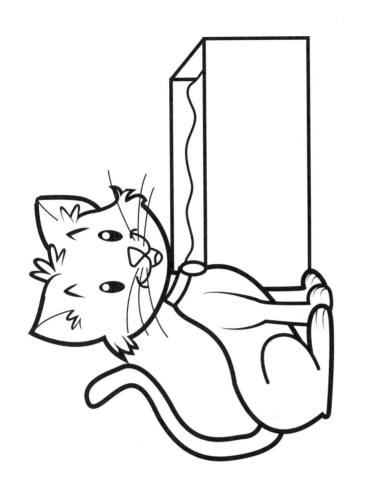

He is out of the box.

He is over the gate.

He can go up the slide.

He can go down the slide.

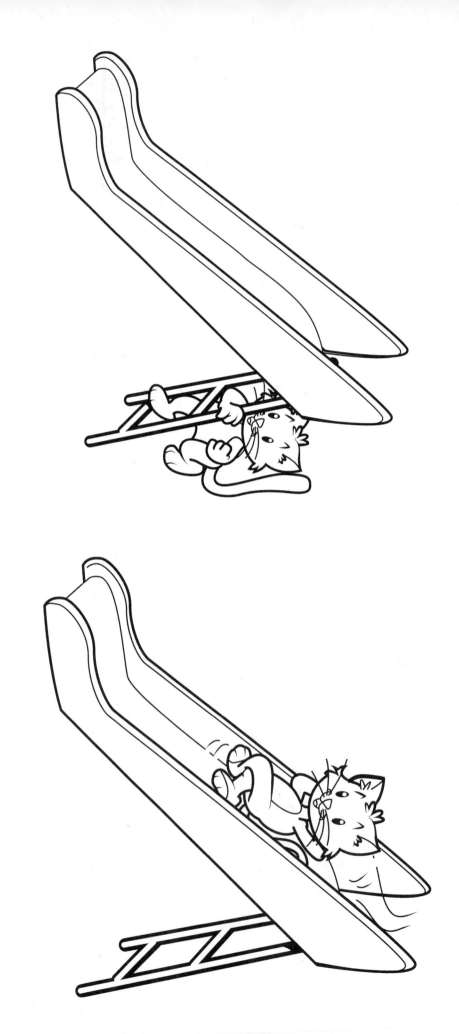

Unit 2 Planner
Letter Recognition

Lesson	Phonemic Awareness	Phonics	Vocabulary	Comprehension and Fluency	Stories, Songs, and Rhymes
Lesson 1 Recognizing *Aa, Bb, Cc, Dd*	**Phoneme Isolation:** Identify the beginning sound in words using the letters *a, b, c, d* **Phoneme Identity:** *apple, ax, alligator bed, book, bell cake, cot, cap door, doll, dig*	Letter Team Match-up with *a, b, c, d* Activity Pages 36–40			**Song:** "ABC Song"
Lesson 2 Recognizing *Ee, Ff, Gg, Hh*	**Phoneme Isolation:** Identify the beginning sound in words using the letters *e, f, g, h* **Phoneme Identity:** *elf, exit, egg fish, fork, fox goat, gas, gum horse, hat, house*	Racetrack Game with *e, f, g, h* Activity Pages 41–45			**Song:** "The Farmer in the Dell"
Lesson 3 Recognizing *Ii, Jj, Kk, Ll*	**Phoneme Isolation:** Identify the beginning sound in words using the letters *i, j, k, l* **Phoneme Identity:** *igloo, inch, ill jog, jump, jam key, king, kitten lemon, lamp, lock*	Name Game with *i, j, k, l* Activity Pages 46–50			**Nursery Rhyme:** "Jack and Jill"
Lesson 4 Recognizing *Mm, Nn, Oo, Pp*	**Phoneme Isolation:** Identify the beginning sound in words using the letters *m, n, o, p* **Phoneme Identity:** *monkey, mat, mop nest, nickel, net octopus, otter, ox pig, pen, piano*	Coin Toss with *m, n, o, p* Activity Pages 51–55			**Story:** "The Three Little Pigs"
Lesson 5 Recognizing *Qq, Rr, Ss, Tt*	**Phoneme Isolation:** Identify the beginning sound in words using the letters *q, r, s, t* **Phoneme Identity:** *quilt, queen, quit rake, rain, rope sock, sink, sun table, tent, tiger*	Word Ladder with *q, r, s, t* Activity Pages 56–60			**Song:** "Six Little Ducks"
Lesson 6 Recognizing *Uu, Vv, Ww, Xx, Yy, Zz*	**Phoneme Isolation:** Identify the beginning sound in words using the letters *u, v, w, x, y, z* **Phoneme Identity:** *up, umpire, umbrella van, vase, violin watch, well, wig box, mix, wax yarn, yolk, yellow zoo, zebra, zipper*	Alphabet Puppets with *u, v, w, x, y, z* Activity Pages 61–68			**Song:** "Yankee Doodle"
Lesson 7 Story: "Look Up!"			*up, sky, way*	Story Pages 69–72	

Phonics, Kindergarten SV 8860-9

Unit 2: Letter Recognition

🐦 Develop Phonemic Awareness

The focus of this unit is to introduce letter shapes so that children can easily recognize partner letters. However, it is recommended that teachers play daily sound games with children to develop attentiveness, listening skills, and initial recognition of the letter sounds.

• **Phoneme Isolation** Show children pictures of a few animals. Ask them to make the sounds that the animals make. Emphasize that each animal makes its own sound. Then show children the letters of the alphabet. Tell them that each of the letters is like the animals because each letter makes its own sound. Explain that we use letters and their sounds to make words. Using the target letters in the planner on page 33, have children practice identifying the beginning sounds of words.

• **Phoneme Identity** As you introduce each letter, say the corresponding group of words listed in the planner on page 33. Have children identify the beginning sound that all three words have in common. Display the target letters and challenge children to identify the letter that makes the beginning sound of the three words.

🔤 Explore Phonics

Use these group activities to help children explore each letter.

• **Letter Team Match-up with *a, b, c, d*** Have eight children form two lines with four in each line. Randomly distribute the letter cards *A, a, B, b, C, c, D, d* to the children in each line. At your signal, have each child in one line locate the child in the opposite line with the partner letter. Have each pair hold up their matching letters and say the letter name. Challenge children to name a word that begins with the sound that their letter makes.

• **Racetrack Game with *e, f, g, h*** Make copies of Master 2 on page 154 and assemble the track. Randomly write one of the target letters in each space of the board using only capital letters. Highlight one space as the starting point. Write lowercase target letters on

index cards, making several for each letter. Provide each group of two players a small toy car as a game marker and the stack of cards. Players take turns drawing a card from the top of the stack. Players who name an object that begins with the same sound as the letter drawn may move to the matching capital letter space. Play until everyone has circled the track.

• **Name Game with *i, j, k, l*** Draw five large houses along the bottom of the chalkboard. Write the capital target letters in four of the houses and leave the fifth house empty. Invite children to name the letter in each house. Have a volunteer write the lowercase letter for each partner letter in the house. Invite children to print their first name in a house if that letter has the same beginning sound as their name. If their name does not begin with any of the target letters, children should print their name in the empty house.

• **Coin Toss with *m, n, o, p*** Copy Master 1 on page 153 and write one of the target letters in each box, making sure to use capital letters in some boxes and lowercase letters in others. Repeat letters until all boxes are filled. Give partner pairs a copy of the grid, a plastic token or coin, and a different colored crayon. Place the grid on the floor and have partners take turns tossing the token or coin on the grid. Children who can name an object that begins with the sound of the letter on which the token lands can color that box. At the end of the allotted time, count to see who has the most boxes colored.

• **Word Ladder with *q, r, s, t*** Place picture cards whose names begin with the target letters on the base of the wall. Provide each member of a small group four or five cards with the target letters written on them, including both capital and lowercase letters. Have children spread the cards with the letters face-down. Choose one child at a time to turn over a card, identify the letter, and tape it above the picture card that has the same initial sound.

• **Alphabet Puppets with *u, v, w, x, y, z*** Provide copies of Master 3 on page 155. Have each member of a small group make six letter puppets. Have them write one of the capital target letters on each puppet. Make cards with the lowercase target letters written on them.

Look Up!

X, Y, Z!

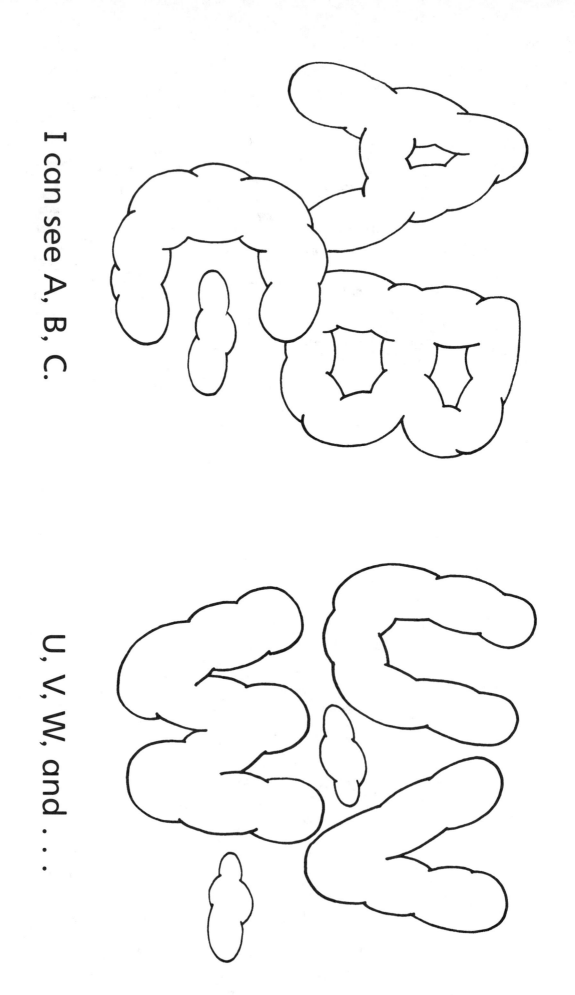

I can see A, B, C.

U, V, W, and . . .

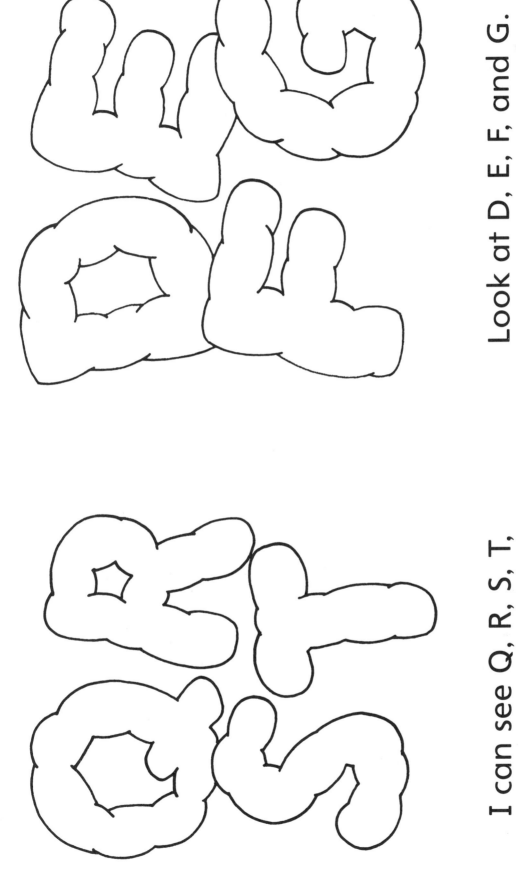

Look at D, E, F, and G.

I can see Q, R, S, T,

Up in the sky H, I, J, K.

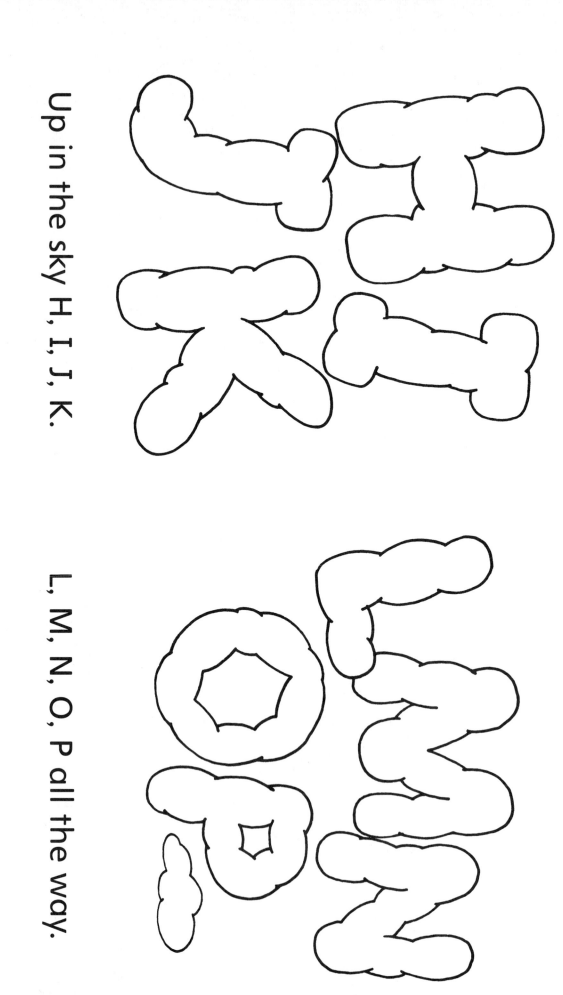

L, M, N, O, P all the way.

Unit 3 Planner
Consonants

Lesson	Phonemic Awareness	Phonics	Vocabulary	Comprehension and Fluency	Stories, Songs, and Rhymes
Lesson 1 Consonants *m, d, f*	**Phoneme Identity:** *mop, mouse, moon dog, desk, dill fan, fox, fish* **Phoneme Segmentation:** *mop, dog, fan*	Word Ladders with *m, d , f* Activity Pages 76–82			**Nursery Rhyme:** "Hey, Diddle, Diddle"
Lesson 2 Consonants *g, b, t*	**Phoneme Identity:** *gum, gas, gate bed, ball, bus top, tub, tag* **Phoneme Segmentation:** *gum, bed, top*	Alphabet Puppets with *g, b, t* Activity Pages 83–89 Rhyme Page 90			**Story:** "The Three Billy Goats Gruff"
Lesson 3 Consonants *s, w, k*	**Phoneme Identity:** *sun, sock, six web, wig, wall kite, key, king* **Phoneme Segmentation:** *sun, web, kite*	Coin Toss with *s, w, k* Activity Pages 91–97			**Song:** "Willoby Walloby Woo"
Lesson 4 Consonants *j, p, n*	**Phoneme Identity:** *jet, jam, jeep pig, pot, pen nest, nut, net* **Phoneme Segmentation:** *jet, pig, nest*	Step-Page Book with *j, p, n* Activity Pages 98–104 Rhyme Page 105			**Nursery Rhyme:** "Peter Piper"
Lesson 5 Consonants *c, h, l*	**Phoneme Identity:** *cat, cup, cot ham, hen, hand log, lid, lock* **Phoneme Segmentation:** *cat, ham, log*	Racetrack Game with *c, h, l* Activity Pages 106–112			**Nursery Rhyme:** "Hickory Dickory Dock"
Lesson 6 Consonants *r, v, y*	**Phoneme Identity:** *rug, robe, rake van, vine, vase yell, yarn, yolk* **Phoneme Segmentation:** *rug, van, yell*	Scavenger Hunt with *r, v, y* Activity Pages 113–119 Rhyme Page 120			**Story:** "Little Red Riding Hood"
Lesson 7 Consonants *z, q, x*	**Phoneme Identity:** *zip, zero, zoo quack, quilt, queen box, ax, six* **Phoneme Segmentation:** *zip, quack, box*	Memory Game with *z, q, x* Activity Pages 121–127			**Song:** "Zippity Doo Dah"
Lesson 8 Story: "Hello, New Room"			*cat, doll, hat, hello, kite, new, room, truck* Activity Page 128	Story Pages 129–132	

Phonics, Kindergarten SV 8860-9

Unit 3: Consonants

Develop Phonemic Awareness

You may wish to introduce the letter sounds using these phonemic awareness techniques before children see the letters.

• **Phoneme Identity** As you introduce each letter, say the corresponding group of words listed in the planner on page 73. Have children identify the sound that all three words have in common. Challenge children to brainstorm words that begin with the same sound, or for the letter *x*, words that end with the same sound.

• **Phoneme Segmentation** Tell children that you will sound out a target word from the planner on page 73. Have them count the sounds they hear. Then have children repeat the phonemes and identify the word. Next, repeat the segmented word and help children write the word or draw a picture of it in their Writer's Dictionary.

Explore Phonics

Use these group activities to help children explore each consonant.

• **Word Ladders with *m, d, f*** Challenge children to draw pictures of objects whose names begin with *m, d,* or *f* or to write the names of those objects on index cards. Have them tape the cards on a wall to form a "ladder."

• **Alphabet Puppets with *g, b, t*** Provide copies of Master 3 on page 155. Have each member of a small group make three letter puppets and write one target letter on each puppet. As you say a word, have children wiggle the puppet that stands for the beginning sound of each word.

• **Coin Toss with *s, w, k*** Make a copy of Master 1 on page 153 and write a target letter in each box. Repeat letters until all boxes are filled. Provide partner pairs with copies of the grid, two plastic tokens or coins, and two different colored crayons. Place the grid on the floor and have partners take turns tossing the token or coin on the grid. Children who can name an object that begins with the same sound of the letter on which the token lands can color that box. Have children continue until all the boxes are colored.

• **Step-Page Book with *j, p, n*** Provide each child with a copy of Master 4 on page 156. Once the books are assembled, write a title for the book on the chalkboard, such as *Fun with J, P, and N.* Invite children to copy the title onto the first page of their book. Then have children write a target letter on each of the remaining pages. Have them draw pictures whose names begin with the target letters on the pages.

• **Racetrack Game with *c, h, l*** Make copies of Master 2 on page 154 and assemble the track. Label one space *Start* and write target letters in the remaining spaces. Provide each group of two players two small toy cars as game markers and a die to move along the game board. Players take turns rolling the die. In order to move forward on the board, players must name an object that begins with the same sound as the target letter on which they landed. Play until everyone has circled the track.

• **Scavenger Hunt with *r, v, y*** Place picture cards whose names begin with the target letters around the room. Provide each team of three children a card with one of the target letters written on it. Have each team look around the room and collect all picture cards whose names begin with their target letter. When the hunt has ended, have each team name the pictures they found.

• **Memory Game with *z, q, x*** Display 10–12 objects or pictures of objects whose names begin with the letters *z* or *q* or end with the letter *x.* Cover the objects and select one target letter. Challenge a child to name as many of the displayed objects as he or she can remember that begin or end with the selected sound. Uncover each object as it is named.

Develop Vocabulary and Meaning

Consonant Words

c: cat	*d:* doll	*h:* hat, hello
k: kite	*n:* new	*r:* room
t: truck		

The following activities will help prepare children for reading the unit story independently. Afterwards, children can complete the vocabulary exercise on page 128.

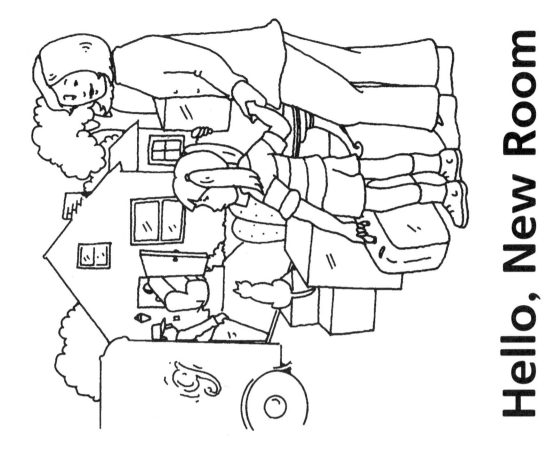

Hello, New Room

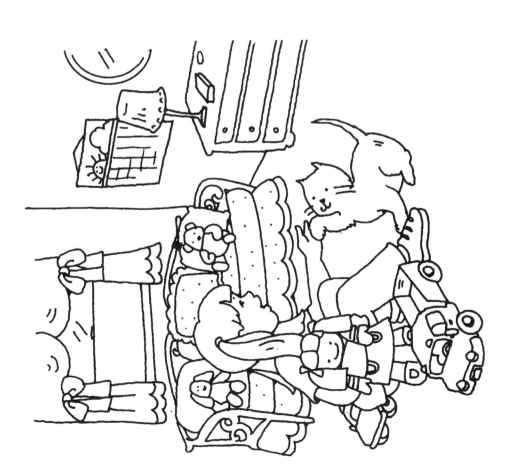

Hello, new room!

Hello, new room.

Hello, truck.

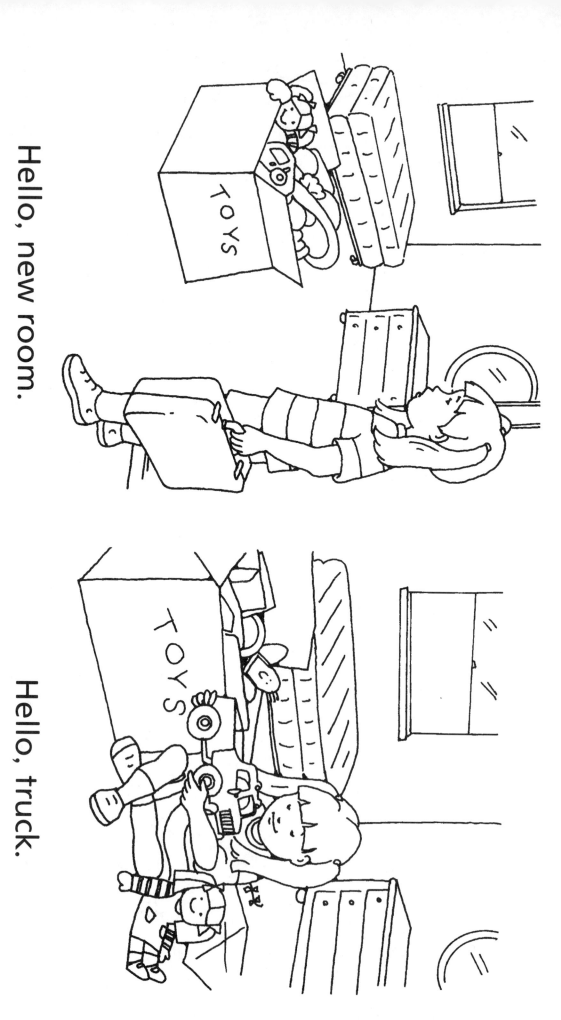

Hello, hat.

Hello, doll.

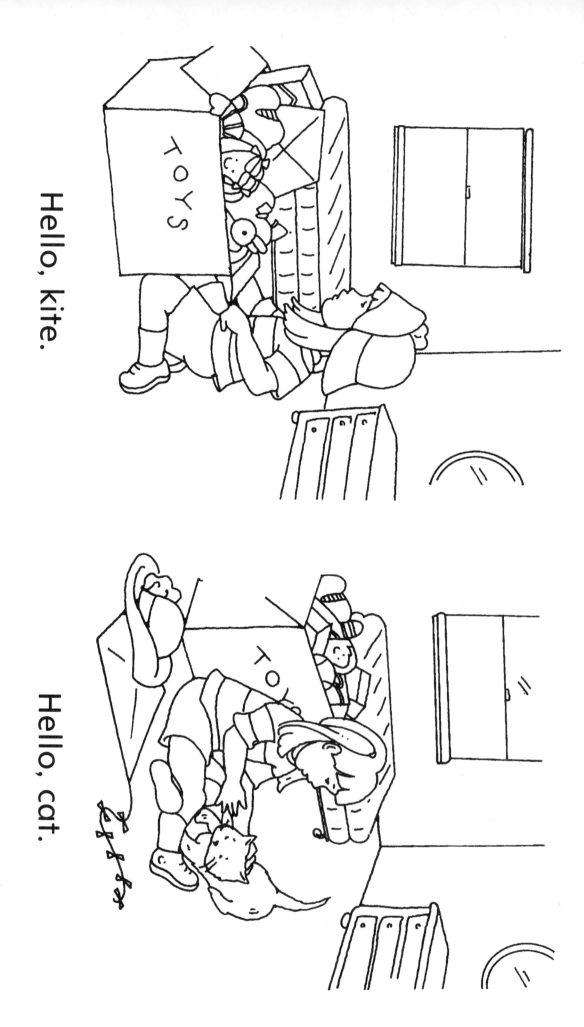

Hello, kite.

Hello, cat.

Unit 4 Planner
Short Vowels

Lesson	Phonemic Awareness	Phonics	Vocabulary	Comprehension and Fluency	Stories, Songs, and Rhymes
Lesson 1 Short Vowel *a*	**Phoneme Identity:** *apple, ax, alligator* **Phoneme Blending:** *map, cat, gas*	Step-Page Book with Medial *a* Activity Pages 136–137			**Song:** "The Ants Go Marching"
Lesson 2 Short Vowel *o*	**Phoneme Identity:** *ox, octopus, otter* **Phoneme Blending:** *pot, box, top*	Memory Game with Medial *o* Activity Pages 138–139			**Song:** "Five Little Speckled Frogs"
Lesson 3 Short Vowel *i*	**Phoneme Identity:** *igloo, inch, insect* **Phoneme Blending:** *lid, mitt, pig*	Rhyming Word Ladder with Medial *i* Activity Pages 140–142			**Nursery Rhyme:** "Itsy Bitsy Spider"
Lesson 4 Short Vowel *u*	**Phoneme Identity:** *umbrella, up, umpire* **Phoneme Blending:** *bug, gum, cut*	Coin Toss with Medial *u* Activity Pages 143–144			**Nursery Rhyme:** "Rub-a-dub-dub"
Lesson 5 Short Vowel *e*	**Phoneme Identity:** *egg, elf, elephant* **Phoneme Blending:** *bed, vet, hen*	Egg Hunt with Medial *e* Activity Pages 145–147			**Story:** "The Little Red Hen"
Lesson 6 Story: "The Bug"			*mug, rug, run, sat* Activity Page 148	Story Pages 149–152	

Phonics, Kindergarten SV 8860-9

🐦 Develop Phonemic Awareness

You may wish to introduce the short vowel sounds using these phonemic awareness techniques before children see the letters.

• **Phoneme Identity** As you introduce each short vowel sound, say the corresponding group of words from the planner on page 133. Have children identify the initial short vowel sound that all three words have in common. Challenge children to brainstorm other words that have the same initial short vowel sound. Write the words on the chalkboard or a chart.

• **Phoneme Blending** Say a sequence of separately spoken phonemes for each of the corresponding group of words from the planner on page 133. Challenge children to combine the phonemes to form a word. Ask them to identify the short vowel sound in each word. You may wish to have them write the word and read it.

🔤 Explore Phonics

Use these group activities to help children explore each vowel sound.

• **Step-Page Book with Medial a** Have children brainstorm words that have the medial short *a* sound. Write the words on the chalkboard. Provide each child with a copy of Master 4 on page 156. Once the books are assembled, have children copy one word from the list on each of the pages of their book. You may wish to read the word list again and challenge the children to listen for the sounds of the words they want to copy. Then have them draw or cut out pictures from magazines that illustrate each word they have selected.

• **Memory Game with Medial o** Display 4 objects or pictures of objects whose names have the medial *o* sound and 4 objects or pictures whose names have other medial vowel sounds. Have children listen for the medial vowel sounds of all objects as you name them. Cover the objects or pictures and challenge volunteers to name an object that has the medial *o* sound. Uncover each object or picture as it is named.

• **Rhyming Word Ladder with Medial i** Draw pictures of medial *i* words (*lid, mitt, pig*) on separate index cards. Tape each picture card along the base of a wall. Challenge children to brainstorm words that rhyme with each of the picture names. As they name a rhyming word, draw a simple picture of it on an index card. Have volunteers select a card and tape it to the appropriate rhyming "ladder."

• **Coin Toss with Medial u** Make a copy of Master 1 on page 153 and write the letter *u* in each box. Provide a copy of the grid, a plastic token or coin, and two different colored crayons for each group of two children. Place the grid on the floor and have partners take turns tossing the token or coin on the grid. The child who can correctly name an object that has the medial *u* sound can color that box. At the end of the allotted time, count to see who has more boxes colored.

• **Egg Hunt with Medial e** Place a basket at the front of the room. Collect 8–10 small pictures of objects whose names have a medial *e* and 4–5 pictures of objects whose names have other medial vowel sounds. Place each picture in a plastic egg and hide the eggs around the room. Have partners hunt for the eggs. Challenge them to open each egg they find and decide if the picture name has a medial *e* sound. If it does have the target sound, they may place the egg in the basket. After the egg hunt, encourage volunteers to open an egg from the basket, name the picture, and verify that the picture name has the medial *e* sound.

📖 Develop Vocabulary and Meaning

Short Vowel Words

a: hat   *o:* hop   *i:* big   *u:* bug   *e:* fell

High-Frequency Words

a, at, can, go, he, in, look, my, on, that, the, see

Story Words

mug, rug, run, sat

The following activities will help prepare children for reading the unit story independently. Afterwards, children can complete the vocabulary exercise on page 148.

- **Match the Sounds** Write the words below on the chalkboard and read them aloud. Circle the medial vowel, name the letter, and repeat the word, stressing the medial vowel sound. Repeat the process and have children echo. Then challenge children to find words in the story that have the same medial letter and vowel sound as the words on the chalkboard.

jam/hat	vest/fell	frog/hop
duck/mug	gift/big	

- **Blend the Words** Say the sounds that make up some of the words below. Have children listen to the sounds and then blend them to say the word.

/b/ /u/ /g/ (bug)	/b/ /i/ /g/ (big)
/h/ /o/ /p/ (hop)	/h/ /a/ /t/ (hat)
/f/ /e/ /l/ /l/ (fell)	/r/ /u/ /n/ (run)

 Read the Story: "The Bug"

Before Reading

Display the cover of the book and read the title aloud. Have children look at the picture on the cover and describe what they see. Have them predict what is going to happen in the story. Ask children to follow along in their books as you read the story to see if their predictions are correct.

During Reading

- **Model Fluency** As you read the story aloud, model using expression for exclamatory sentences and for showing a character's feelings.

- **Model Decoding** You may wish to model how to decode words using phonics sounds.

- **Model Comprehension** Model how to understand a story by looking at the illustration first. Use a blank card to cover the words of the story and have children tell what is happening in the illustration. Ask them how the illustration can help the reader to understand a story word.

After Reading

Have children find and read the words or phrases in the story that answer the following questions.

What did the bug sit on? (hat, rug)
What did the bug fall into? (mug)
How did the bug move? (hop, run)

Did the mother and the girl like the bug? How do you know? (Possible answer: The mother and the girl liked the bug because they were smiling at the end of the story.)

 Reread the Story

- **Oral Reading** Talk about point of view in the story, and help children understand that the lines of the story are what the girl says to her mother. Then invite children to take turns reading the story aloud, each reading a line. Encourage them to read the lines the way they think the girl might have said them.

- **Fluent Reading** Have partners turn to page 2. Point out that the sentence ends with an exclamation point. Model how to read the sentence with appropriate expression. Invite partners to rehearse the sentence to show expression.

- **Retell the Story** Ask children to tell what happens in the story in their own words. Encourage them to tell the story as a narrative. That is, they should tell what the bug does and what the girl and her mother do, too.

 Connect the Story to Writing

- **Shared Writing** Review the three lines from the story that tell places where the bug sat or fell. Invite children to use the pattern of the story sentences to tell other places where the bug might go. Write all the sentences children suggest on chart paper. Then have each child choose a sentence and draw a picture to illustrate it.

Support ESOL Learners

Children who are learning English may have difficulty producing some vowel sounds.

 At Home

Encourage children to read "The Bug" with someone at home. After reading, suggest they discuss what they would do if a bug appeared on their kitchen table.

Name_____

Listen for a

Aa

■ Have children color the pictures whose names have the same **a** sound as **apple**.

Unit 4: Short Vowel *a*
Phonics, Kindergarten SV 8860-9

Name_____

Hear and Write a

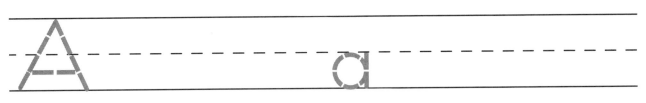

■ Have children trace and write **A** and **a**. Then have them write **a** under each picture whose name has the same **a** sound as **apple**.

Unit 4: Short Vowel *a*
Phonics, Kindergarten SV 8860-9

Name _____

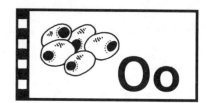

Listen for o

■ Have children color the pictures whose names have the same **o** sound as **olives**.

Name _____

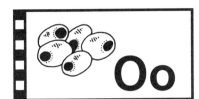

Hear and Write o

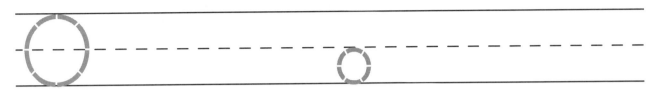

■ Have children trace and write **O** and **o**. Then have them write **o** under each picture whose name has the same **o** sound as **olives**.

Name

Listen for i

■ Have children color the pictures whose names have the same **i** sound as **igloo**.

Unit 4: Short Vowel *i*
Phonics, Kindergarten SV 8860-9

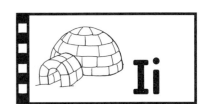

Ii

Hear and Write **i**

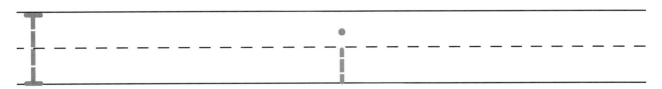

■ Have children trace and write **I** and **i**. Then have them write **i** under each picture whose name has the same **i** sound as **igloo**.

Name_____

Review a, o, i

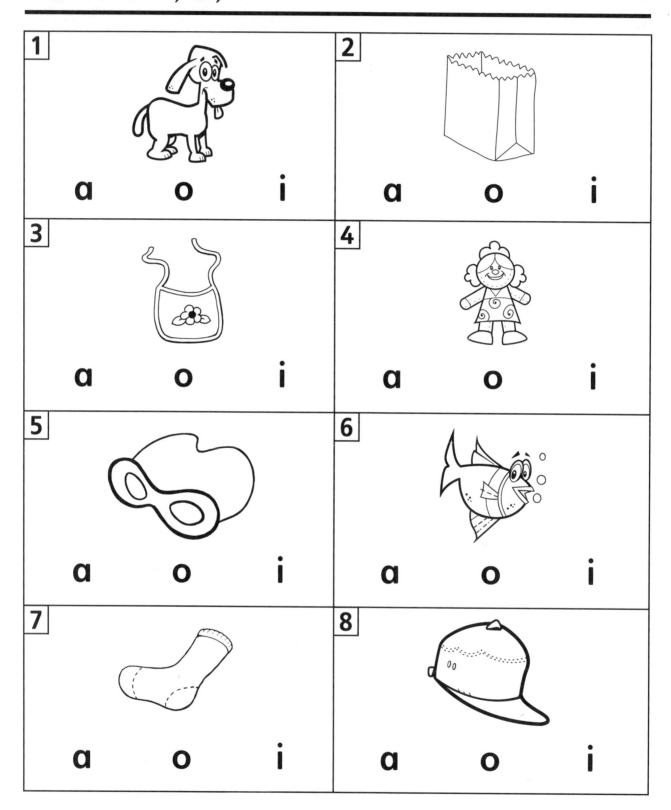

1		2	
a	o	i	a	o	i

1 a o i

2 a o i

3 a o i

4 a o i

5 a o i

6 a o i

7 a o i

8 a o i

■ Have children circle the letter that stands for the vowel sound in each picture name.

Name _____

Listen for u

■ Have children color the pictures whose names have the same **u** sound as **umbrella**.

Name_____

Hear and Write u

U - - - - - - - - - - - - - - - - - - U - - - - - - -

_ _ _ _ _ _	_ _ _ _ _ _	_ _ _ _ _ _
_ _ _ _ _ _	_ _ _ _ _ _	_ _ _ _ _ _

■ Have children trace and write **U** and **u**. Then have them write **u** under each picture whose name has the same **u** sound as **umbrella**.

Listen for e

■ Have children color the pictures whose names have the same **e** sound as **egg**.

Name_____

Hear and Write e

E - e - - - - - - - - - - - - - - -

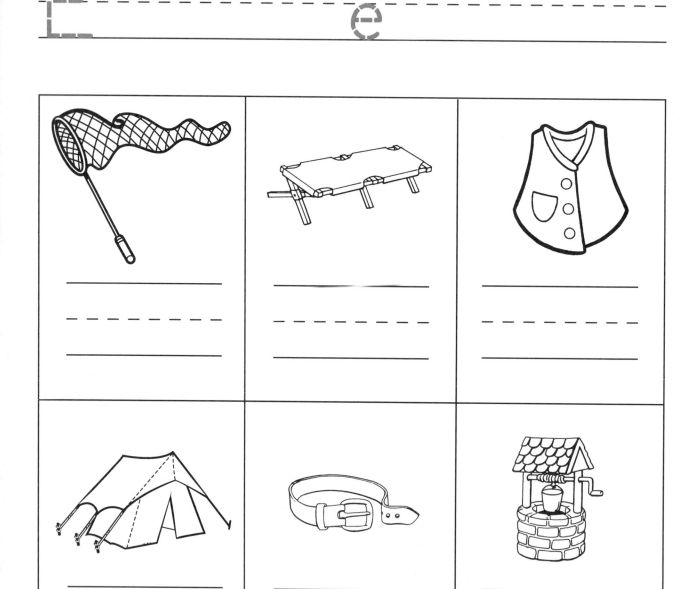

■ Have children trace and write **E** and **e**. Then have them write **e** under each picture whose name has the same **e** sound as **egg**.

Name_____

Review u and e

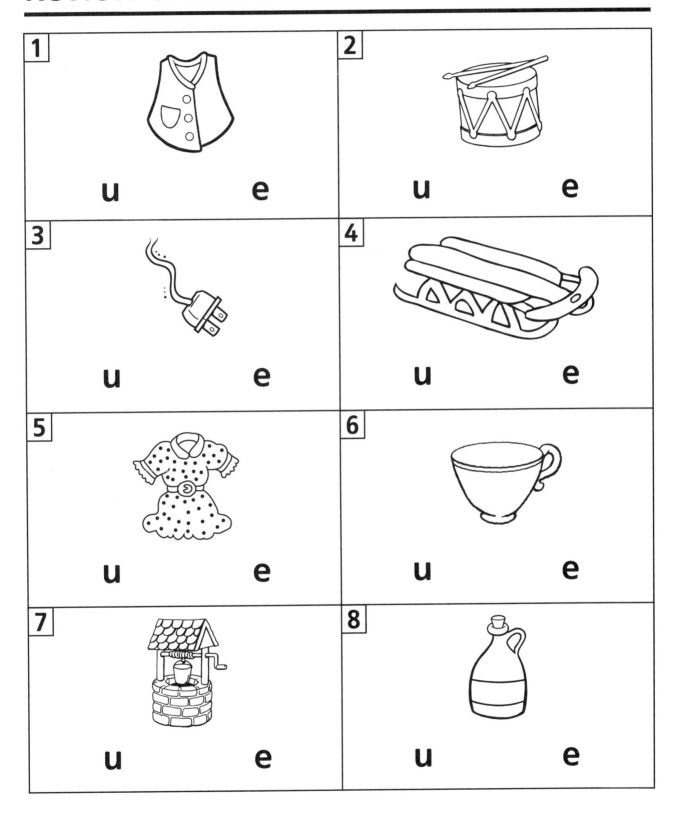

1 u e	**2** u e
3 u e	**4** u e
5 u e	**6** u e
7 u e	**8** u e

■ Have children circle the letter that stands for the vowel sound in each picture name.

Vocabulary

1

My _____ is red.

mug

run

2

Put on the _____.

bug

hat

3

The bug _____.

sat

rug

4

The bug can _____.

hop

mug

5

I _____ on the rug.

hat

fell

6

The _____ is soft.

run

rug

■ Have children read each sentence. Then have them circle and write the word that completes each sentence.

The Bug

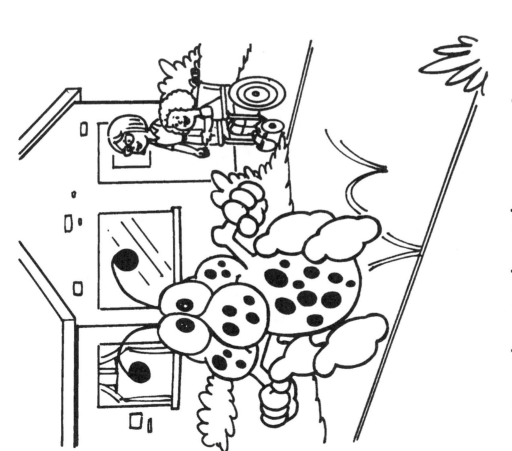

Look at that bug go!

A big bug!

He can run.

The bug sat on my hat.

The bug can hop.

The bug fell in my mug.

The bug sat on my rug.

Name_____

Grid

Racetrack Game Board

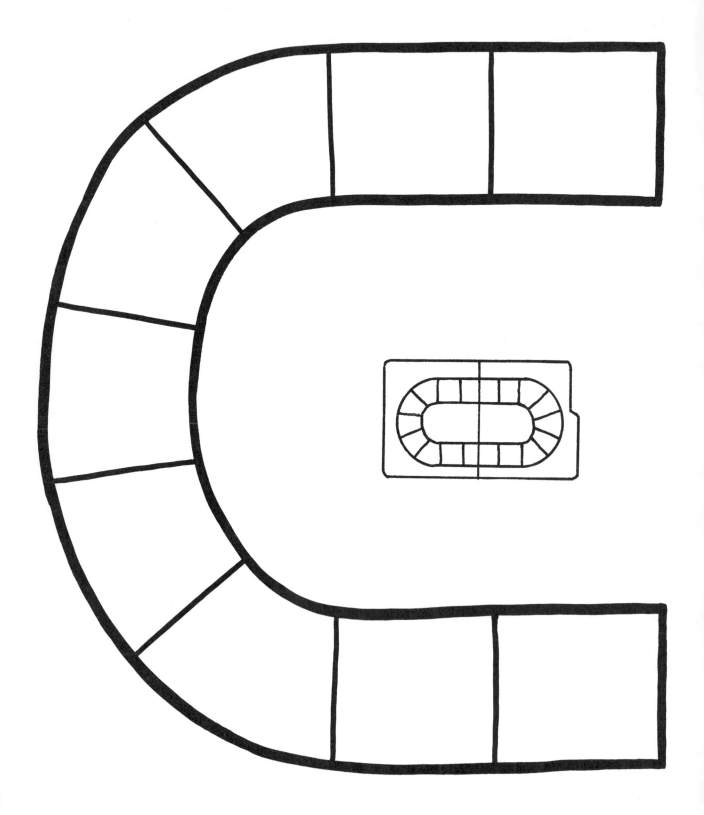

Name

Finger Puppets

1. Cut.   **2.** Draw or write.    **3.** Tape.   **4.** Wear.

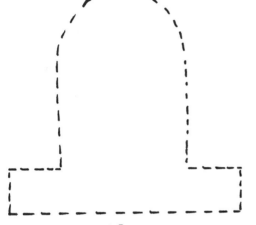
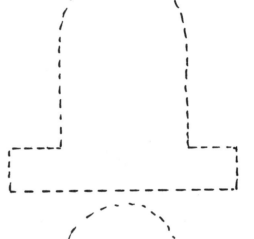
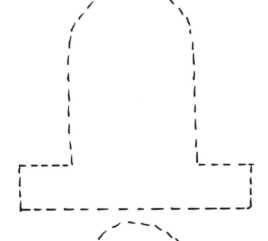
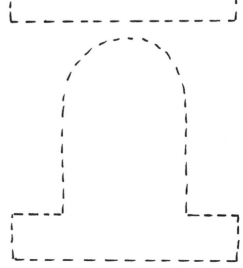

Blackline Master 3

Phonics, Kindergarten SV 8860-9

Step-Page Book

1. Cut out the four pages.

2. Lay the pages one on top of the other.

3. Bind the pages at the top.

Name_____

Writer's Dictionary

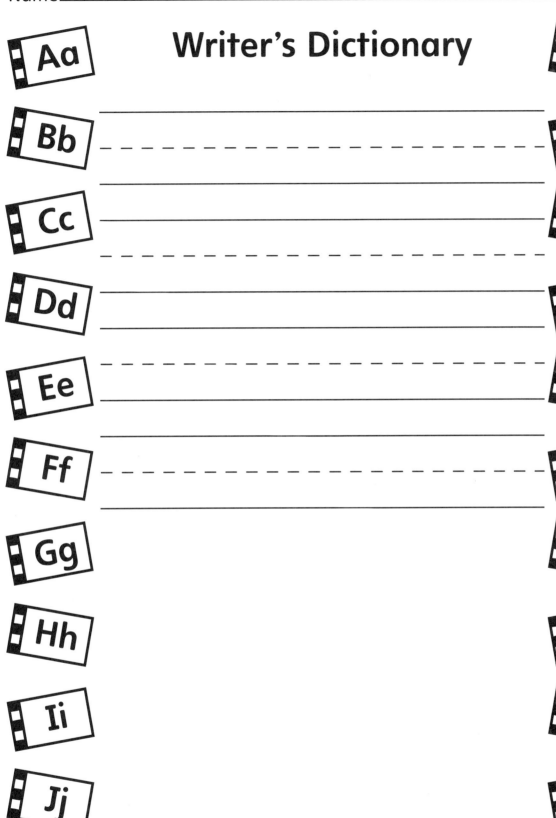

Phonics Plus, Kindergarten
Answer Key

Page 14

Check students' work.

Page 15

Color the two baseballs.

Color the two bears.

Color the two cars.

Page 16

Color the bowl with sausages in it.

Color the bowl with CAT written on it.

Page 17

Color the girl flying a kite.

Color the boy sitting on the shoe.

Color the boy picking a flower.

Color the boy behind the bush.

Page 18

Color the three children inside the cars.

Page 19

Draw wheels on the car.

Draw windows on the house.

Draw a shirt with a heart on the bear.

Page 20

Circle the third nest.

Circle the second rain cloud.

Circle the fourth flower.

Page 21

Color the swing, slide, and sandbox.

Color the crayon box, scissors, and glue.

Color the baseball, bat, and mitt.

Page 22

Check students' work.

Page 23

Check students' work.

Page 24

Check students' work.

Page 25

Fish, sea horse, octopus.

Page 26

Check students' work.

Page 27

Sail: whale, nail, snail.

Lock: clock, rock, sock.

Page 28

1. c
2. b
3. s
4. g

Page 36

Check students' work.

Page 37

Check students' work.

Page 38

Check students' work.

Page 39

Check students' work.

Page 40

Color balloons with letters Aa, Cc, Bb, Dd.

Page 41

Check students' work.

Page 42

Check students' work.

Page 43

Check students' work.

Page 44

Check students' work.

Page 45

Color elephants with letters Ee, Ff, Hh, Gg.

Page 46

Check students' work.

Page 47

Check students' work.

Page 48

Check students' work.

Page 49

Check students' work.

Page 50

Color kites with letters Ll, Kk, Ii, Jj.

Page 51

Check students' work.

Page 52

Check students' work.

Page 53

Check students' work.

Page 54

Check students' work.

Page 55

Color penguins with letters Nn, Mm, Oo, Pp.

Page 56

Check students' work.

Page 57

Check students' work.

Page 58

Check students' work.

Page 59

Check students' work.

Page 60

Color rabbits with letters
Qq, Ss, Rr, Tt.

Page 61

Check students' work.

Page 62

Check students' work.

Page 63

Check students' work.

Page 64

Check students' work.

Page 65

Check students' work.

Page 66

Check students' work.

Page 67

Color umbrellas with letters
Ww, Xx, Zz, Yy, Uu, Vv.

Page 68

1. Mm, Aa, Kk
2. zZ, sS, nN
3. Vv, Ww, Yy
4. Pp, Rr, Ww
5. hH, bB, jJ
6. Ee, Ll, Ff
7. Dd, Cc, Gg
8. Oo, Qq, Uu

Page 76

Color monkey, mask,
mouse, milk, money, mat.

Page 77

Map, monkey, mitten,
mug.

Page 78

Color duck, doll, dishes,
desk, door, deer.

Page 79

Doll, drum, door, dress.

Page 80

Color fish, fox, football,
frog, fork, feather.

Page 81

Five, fire, foot, fox.

Page 82

Mm–mop, mouse, milk.

Dd–dog, doll, desk.

Ff–fox, fan.

Page 83

Color game, gate, guitar,
goat, girl, gum.

Page 84

Guitar, gum, game, gate,
goat.

Page 85

Color boat, banana, bike,
belt, bell, basket, bone.

Page 86

Bike, box, balloon, bat, bed.

Page 87

Color telephone, tape, tent,
tub, toothpaste, tiger, top.

Page 88

Television, toe, table, tag,
tub.

Page 89

Gg–goat, gum.

Bb–bike, bird.

Tt–tent, tub.

Page 90

Color goat, boat, dog, frog.

Page 91

Color seal, soap, sun,
sandwich, sock, six, saw.

Page 92

Sandwich, sun, saw, soap,
seal.

Page 93

Color watermelon, web,
well, window, wagon, wig,
walrus.

Page 94

Window, walrus, wave,
watermelon, wagon.

Page 95

Color kangaroo, kitten, key,
king, kick, kite.

Page 96

King, kick, kite, kangaroo,
key.

Page 97

Ss–sun, sandwich.

Ww–wagon, window.

Kk–king, key.

Page 98

Color jack-in-the-box, jug,
jar, jet, jump, jacket.

Page 99

Jump, jacks, jacket, jar,
jack-in-the-box.

Page 100

Color puppet, pot, pear,
purse, peas, pencil, piano,
pan.

Page 101

Pin, peas, puppet, purse,
pipe.

Page 102

Color nail, nose, net, nurse,
needle, nine, newspaper.

Page 103

Nuts, numbers, newspaper,
nose, nest.

Page 104

1. j
2. p
3. n
4. p
5. n
6. j
7. j
8. p

Page 105

Kite–light; star–car; wagon–dragon.

Page 106

Color car, comb, cup, candle, cap, cane, can.

Page 107

Carrot, candle, cot, cap, cane.

Page 108

Color horse, ham, house, hose, hand, hammer, hen.

Page 109

Heart, horse, hair, hammer, hook.

Page 110

Color lion, lips, ladder, lamp, lizard, leg, log.

Page 111

Lizard, lid, lock, lion, log.

Page 112

Cc–carrot, cup.

Hh–house, hat.

Ll–lamp, log.

Page 113

Color rope, rug, rabbit, robe, rain, ring, raccoon.

Page 114

Rainbow, ring, rope, robe.

Page 115

Color van, violin, vacuum, valentine, vine, vase, volcano.

Page 116

Valentine, vine, violin, van, vacuum.

Page 117

Color yoyo, yolk, yawn, yard.

Page 118

Yolk, yarn, yawn, yoyo, yard.

Page 119

r–rug, ring.

v–van.

y–yoyo, yawn.

Page 120

Put an X on dog and cow.

Color horse, lion, and cat.

Page 121

Color zoo, zigzag, zebra, zero.

Page 122

Zebra, zigzag, zero, zipper, zoo.

Page 123

Color quack, quilt, question mark, quarter.

Page 124

Quarter, quilt, queen, quack, question mark.

Page 125

Color box, ox, six, fox, wax.

Page 126

Ox, box, six, fox, ax.

Page 127

1. green   6. red
2. red   7. red
3. purple   8. green
4. purple   9. purple
5. green

Page 128

1. kite   4. doll
2. hat   5. truck
3. cat

Page 136

Color gas, cap, can, ham, bat.

Page 137

Mask, hand, mat, gas.

Page 138

Color box, sock, mop, doll, cot, top.

Page 139

Frog, top, sock, cot.

Page 140

Color fish, mitt, wig, pig, bib, lid.

Page 141

Chick, pig, fish, dishes.

Page 142

1. o   5. a
2. a   6. i
3. i   7. o
4. o   8. a

Page 143

Color brush, duck, plug, drum, cup, jug.

Page 144

Rug, truck, drum, duck.

Page 145

Color sled, nest, web, dress, bell, desk.

Page 146

Net, vest, tent, belt, well.

Page 147

1. e   5. e
2. u   6. u
3. u   7. e
4. e   8. u

Page 148

1. mug   4. hop
2. hat   5. fell
3. sat   6. rug

Answer Key

Phonics, Kindergarten SV 8860-9